MACHINES ★ AT WORK

FIRE TRUCKS

BY CYNTHIA ROBERTS

THE CHILD'S WORLD® • MANKATO, MINNESOTA

The Child's World®

Published in the United States of America by The Child's World®
1980 Lookout Drive • Mankato, MN 56003-1705
800-599-READ • www.childsworld.com

PHOTO CREDITS
© Corbis: 20
© David M. Budd Photography: cover, 2, 4, 7, 8, 16, 19
© iStockphoto.com/James Steidl: 11
© iStockphoto.com/Jon Stephenson: 12
© iStockphoto.com/Nick Schlax: 3
© Kelly-Mooney Photography/Corbis: 15

ACKNOWLEDGMENTS
The Child's World®: Mary Berendes, Publishing Director;
Katherine Stevenson, Editor

The Design Lab: Kathleen Petelinsek, Design and Page Production

LIBRARY OF CONGRESS CATALOGING-IN-PUBLICATION DATA
Roberts, Cynthia, 1960–
  Fire trucks / by Cynthia Roberts.
      p. cm. — (Machines at work)
  Includes bibliographical references and index.
  ISBN 1-59296-831-7 (library bound : alk. paper)
  1. Fire engines—Juvenile literature. I. Title. II. Series.
  TH9372.R626 2007
  628.9'259—dc22   2006023354

 # Contents

This huge fire truck is pulling out of the station. Fire stations need big doors!

What are fire trucks?

Fire trucks are special kinds of trucks. They are used for putting out fires. They are used for other kinds of **emergencies**, too.

What do fire trucks look like?

Fire trucks are big. Most fire trucks are painted bright colors. Many of them are bright red. Some are yellow. Bright colors make the trucks easy to see.

Most fire trucks have the town's name on them. This one is from Seattle.

Fire trucks can be loud! The driver needs to talk to other firefighters. He wears a headset. It helps him hear and talk over the noise.

Where does the driver ride?

The driver sits in the **cab** of the truck. The cab has lots of **controls** for running the truck. It has places for other firefighters to sit, too.

How does a fire truck move?

Fire trucks move like other trucks. An **engine** gives them power. The engine burns **diesel fuel**. The engine's power moves the truck's big wheels. The driver uses a steering wheel to turn the truck.

10

This fire truck is racing down the street.

siren

flashing light

Other cars must pull over when a fire truck is coming.

Fire trucks must get to emergencies quickly. They need to let other drivers know they are coming—fast! They have bright flashing lights. They also have loud **sirens** and horns.

13

Are there different kinds of fire trucks?

There are many kinds of fire trucks. They do different kinds of jobs. Pumpers spray lots of water. Some pumpers carry big tanks full of water. They also carry hoses and tools for fighting fires. They carry masks and air for the firefighters to breathe.

14

The water from the hoses comes out fast! It can take several firefighters to hold each hose.

This ladder truck can take firefighters over 300 feet (91 m) high!

Other fire trucks are made for reaching high places. Their long ladders can reach high windows and rooftops. Some have **platforms** where firefighters can stand. These trucks carry firefighting tools, too.

Rescue trucks help save people's lives. They rescue people from fires, floods, car crashes, and other dangers. They carry tools for freeing people who are trapped. They carry supplies for helping people who are hurt.

Jaws of Life

This rescue truck has the Jaws of Life. These tools help free people who are trapped.

Firefighters are high above this burning building. They are spraying water on the fire.

Are fire trucks important?

Fire trucks are very important. Firefighters face many dangers. Fire trucks help them do their jobs better and more safely. Fire trucks save lives every day!

 # Glossary

cab (KAB) A machine's cab is the area where the driver sits.

controls (kun-TROHLZ) Controls are parts that people use to run a machine.

diesel fuel (DEE-sul fyool) Diesel fuel is a heavy oil that is burned to make power.

emergencies (ee-MUR-junt-seez) Emergencies are times of danger, when people must act quickly.

engine (EN-jun) An engine is a machine that makes something move.

platforms (PLAT-formz) Platforms are raised, flat areas.

rescue (RESS-kyoo) To rescue people is to save them from danger.

sirens (SY-runz) Sirens make loud noises to let people know there is danger.

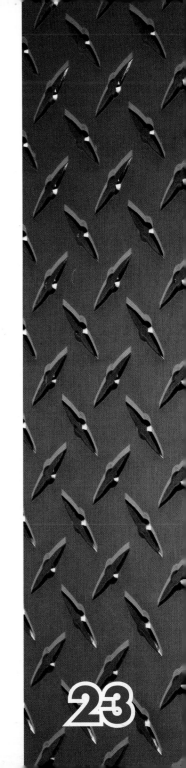

 Books

Bingham, Caroline. *Fire Truck*. New York: DK Publishing, 2003.

Boucher, Jerry. *Fire Truck Nuts and Bolts*. Minneapolis, MN: Carolrhoda Books, 1993.

Marston, Hope Irvin. *Fire Trucks*. New York: Cobblehill Books, 1996.

Slater, Teddy, and Tom LaPadula (illustrator). *All Aboard Fire Trucks*. New York: Platt & Munk, 1991.

Web Sites

Visit our Web site for lots of links about fire trucks:
http://www.childsworld.com/links
Note to parents, teachers, and librarians: We routinely check our Web links to make sure they're safe, active sites—so encourage your readers to check them out!

 # Index

 # About the Author

Even as a child, Cynthia Roberts knew she wanted to be a writer. She is always working to involve kids in reading and writing, and she loves spending time in the children's section of the library ⬛ bookstore. Cynthia enjoys gardening, traveling, and having fun with friends and family.

lish Donut